LIVES AND TIMES

Bach

Wendy Lynch

Heinemann Library
Chicago, Illinois

© 2001 Reed Educational & Professional Publishing
Published by Heinemann Library,
an imprint of Reed Educational & Professional Publishing,
Chicago, Illinois

Customer Service 888-454-2279
Visit our website at www.heinemannlibrary.com

Designed by Visual Image
Illustrations by Sally Barton
Originated by Dot Gradations
Printed and bound in Hong Kong/China

04 03 02
10 9 8 7 6 5 4

Library of Congress Cataloging-in-Publication Data
Lynch, Wendy, 1945-

Bach / Wendy Lynch.

p. cm. – (Lives and times)

Includes bibliographical references and index.

Summary: A simple biography of the man who composed such musical works as the "Brandenburg Concertos."

ISBN 1-57572-214-3 (library binding)

1. Bach, Johann Sebastian, 1685-1750 Juvenile literature.
2. Composers—Germany Biography Juvenile literature. [1. Bach, Johann Sebastian, 1685-1750. 2. Composers.] 1. Title.
II. Series: Lives and times (Des Plaines, Ill.)
ML3930.B2L96 2000
780.92—dc21
[B]
99-37330
CIP

Acknowledgments
The Publishers would like to thank the following for permission to reproduce photographs: AKG London, pp. 16, 17, 18, 22, 23; Mary Evans Picture Library, p. 19; NASA/Science Photo Library, p. 21; Yiorgos Nikiteas, p. 21.

Cover photograph reproduced with permission of e.t. archive.

Every effort has been made to contact copyright holders of any material reproduced in this book. Any omissions will be rectified in subsequent printings if notice is given to the publisher.

Some words are shown in bold, **like this.** You can find out what they mean by looking in the glossary.

Bach

Author: Lynch, Wendy.
Reading Level: 3.2 LG
Point Value: 0.5
ACCELERATED READER QUIZ# 48479

Contents

Part One

Johann Sebastian Bach was born in Germany on March 21, 1685. Bach's father taught him to play the violin and **viola** as soon as his hands were big enough.

Bach started going to school when he was seven years old. He learned **Latin**, history, and math. Bach also sang in a **choir** in church.

When Bach was nine, both his parents died. He went to live with his oldest brother. His brother taught him to play the organ and to make up his own music. This is called **composing**.

Bach was a very good organ player. His little finger was as strong as his **index finger** and could move as fast. This meant he could play fast music without making a mistake.

When Bach was eighteen, he began to earn money by playing music. He began **composing** and playing music for rich and important people. These people were called **patrons**.

Bach's first patron was a duke. For the duke's birthday, Bach wrote a piece of music called "Sheep May Safely **Graze.**"

This music was written with words so that it could be sung.

Bach married his cousin Maria Barbara in 1707. They had seven children, but three of them died. Bach wrote a book of music for his children called The Little Organ Book.

In 1717, Bach began to work for another **patron**, Prince Leopold. The prince loved music. He gave Bach and his family rooms in the palace.

In 1720, Bach's wife Maria Barbara died suddenly. In 1721, Bach married Anna Magdalena. She was a talented singer. They had thirteen children, but seven of them died when they were young.

Bach became head of a music school.
Bach and his students played **concerts** in cafés. Bach wrote the "Coffee **Cantata**" for one of these concerts.

In 1741, Bach visited the palace of King Frederick in Berlin, Germany. Bach played for the king and later wrote some music especially for him.

By 1750, Bach was not doing much work because he could not see very well. Bach died on July 28, 1750. He was 65 years old.

Part Two

We can visit the house where Bach was born. Now it is a museum. In the house, you can see the musical instruments Bach played when he was a boy.

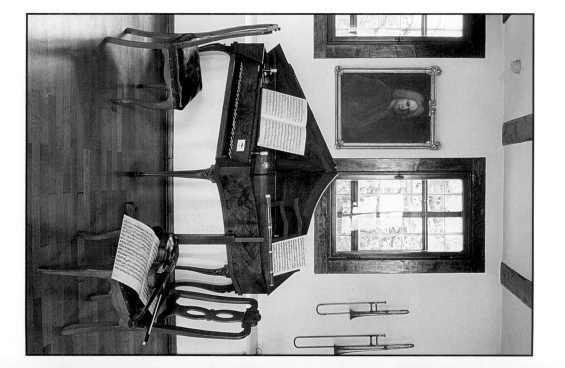

You can visit the church in Leipzig, Germany, where Bach used to play the organ. Bach was buried here.

We can still read Bach's letters today.
This letter was written on October 28,
1730, when Bach was 45 years old.

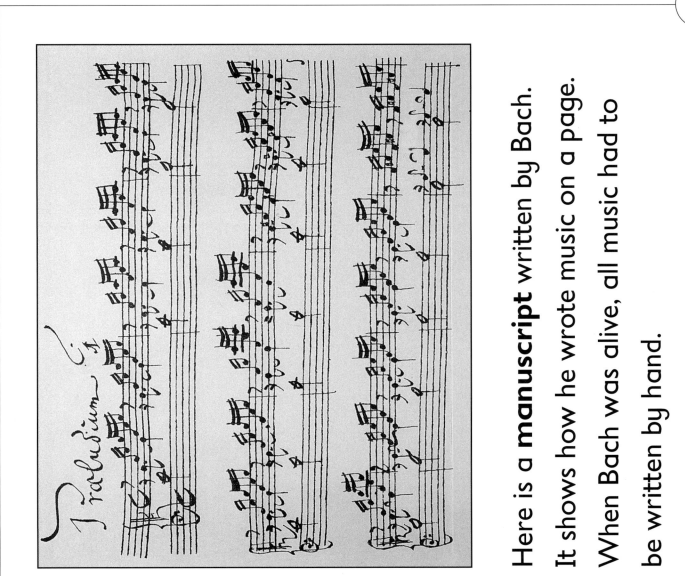

Here is a **manuscript** written by Bach.

It shows how he wrote music on a page.

When Bach was alive, all music had to

be written by hand.

You can listen to Bach's music on a CD or on the radio. This is a CD of Bach's *Brandenburg* **Concertos.**

NAXOS

J. S. BACH
Brandenburg Concertos
Nos. 4, 5 & 6
BWV 1049 - 1051
Capella Istropolitana
Bohdan Warchal

DDD
8.550048

When the Voyager spacecraft was sent into space in 1977, **a recording** of Bach's *Brandenburg Concertos* was put inside it. If there is life on another planet, people there may hear Bach's music.

Paintings show us what Bach looked like. This one was painted when Bach was 35 years old. Many men wore powdered wigs in those days.

You can still see this statue in memory of Bach in Eisenach, Germany. He is holding some music. The statue shows us that Bach and his music are still remembered.

Glossary

cantata short piece of music for voice and instruments

choir group of singers. You say *kw-ire*.

compose to make up music or singers

concert public show by musicians

concerto piece of music in three parts, often for one instrument and an orchestra. You say *con-chair-toe*.

graze the way cows and sheep eat

index finger finger you point with, next to your thumb

Latin language spoken in ancient Rome

manuscript anything written by hand. You say *man-you-script*.

patron someone who gives money or support to a person or group. You say *pay-tron*.

recording piece of music stored on tape or disc

viola instrument like a violin

Index

More Books to Read

Greene, Carol. *Johann Sebastian Bach: Great Man of Music.* Danbury, Conn.: Children's Press, 1993.

Rachlin, Ann. *Bach.* Hauppage, N.Y.: Barron's Educational Series, Inc., 1992.